Retirement
Journal

Adventure Awaits!

What are your plans for retirement? I'm sure you've spent time on the financial plans for your retirement, but what do you plan to actually do with all that free time?

Most adults concentrate their time and energy into their youth and middle age life plans; careers, kids, housing, fitness, but few do more than plan financially for their retirement.

Retirement can be anything you want it to be! Maybe you want to travel the world, go on adventures and explore. You might be happiest spending lots of time with your grandkids and taking cooking or yoga classes. Or maybe you want to start a new hobby/business. Just as in the rest of our lives, we are most successful when we make goals and plans.

Use this journal to capture adventures and activities you would like to embark on. Enjoy!

50 Retirement Adventure Ideas

Need some inspiration? Here are some examples to get you started:

1. Go deep sea fishing or whale watching
2. Go to a remote island or location
3. Go snorkeling
4. Swim with dolphins, stingrays or sharks
5. Watch a volcano erupt
6. See the northern lights
7. Watch the sunrise and sunset in the same day
8. Visit every continent
9. Complete a corn maze
10. Go indoor skydiving
11. Take a helicopter tour
12. Learn a magic trick or how to juggle
13. Visit 50 US states – do the same thing in each state (take a picture next to each state tree, try foods special to that state, or visit one of the state parks)
14. Ride a gondola in Italy
15. Attend a pro sporting event, ballet or show
16. Ride in a hot air balloon
17. Attend a major festival or event (Art, Mardi Gras, New Year's Eve, Burning Man)
18. Do all the tourist attractions in your area
19. Visit the places where you or your parents were born
20. Take cooking classes
21. Enroll in a nutrition class
22. Take yoga or other exercise classes
23. Learn to play a new sport (Frisbee golf, pickle ball)
24. Go on a Safari
25. Stay at a Bed & Breakfast
26. Ride an elephant or camel
27. Teach! You can teach adult education classes, local library classes or at a community college or university
28. Volunteer your expertise to small businesses through SCORE (Service Corps of Retired Executives)
29. Mentor or volunteer at local high schools
30. Visit the seven wonders of the world

31. Write a book, an article, a blog, give a Ted Talk
32. Start a Facebook group, website or a YouTube channel with your interests
33. Write a children's book to teach children or teens more about what you know best
34. Learn a new language – focus on conversational learning and make plans to travel somewhere to use it
35. Learn how to ballroom dance, line dance or do tai chi
36. Learn how to sing, draw, or play an instrument
37. Take an adult education class or classes in different subjects that interest you
38. Let go of a floating lantern
39. Join a book club, wine club or some other club of your interests
40. Research and document your family tree
41. Research different cultures or areas as you visit them
42. Connect with long lost friends or relatives
43. Go on a river cruise
44. Join your local senior center or recreation center and attend group activities
45. Go on an overnight train trip
46. Visit a haunted mansion
47. Visit a castle
48. Participate in a color run/walk or a 5K
49. Horseback ride on the beach
50. Make something artistic (pottery, woodwork, sculpture, painting)

Adventure	Page	Done!
		☐
		☐
		☐
		☐
		☐
		☐
		☐
		☐
		☐
		☐
		☐
		☐
		☐
		☐
		☐
		☐
		☐
		☐
		☐
		☐
		☐
		☐
		☐

Adventure	Page	Done!
		☐
		☐
		☐
		☐
		☐
		☐
		☐
		☐
		☐
		☐
		☐
		☐
		☐
		☐
		☐
		☐
		☐
		☐
		☐
		☐
		☐
		☐
		☐

Adventure	Page	Done!
		☐
		☐
		☐
		☐
		☐
		☐
		☐
		☐
		☐
		☐
		☐
		☐
		☐
		☐
		☐
		☐
		☐
		☐
		☐
		☐
		☐
		☐
		☐

Adventure	Page	Done!
		☐
		☐
		☐
		☐
		☐
		☐
		☐
		☐
		☐
		☐
		☐
		☐
		☐
		☐
		☐
		☐
		☐
		☐
		☐
		☐
		☐
		☐

Date Completed: _____

Overall Rating: ☆ ☆ ☆ ☆ ☆

Description:

_____

_____

_____

_____

_____

Why I wanted to do this:

_____

_____

_____

Thoughts/Memories:

_____

_____

_____

_____

_____

_____

_____

_____

_____

_____

_____

_____

≫≫⟶ ≫≫⟶ | ≫≫⟶ ≫≫⟶

Date Completed:_____

Overall Rating: ☆ ☆ ☆ ☆ ☆

Description:

_____
_____
_____
_____
_____

Why I wanted to do this:

_____
_____
_____

Thoughts/Memories:

_____
_____
_____
_____
_____
_____
_____
_____
_____
_____
_____
_____
_____

Date Completed:_____

Overall Rating: ☆ ☆ ☆ ☆ ☆

Description:

_____
_____
_____
_____
_____

Why I wanted to do this:

_____
_____
_____

Thoughts/Memories:

_____
_____
_____
_____
_____
_____
_____
_____
_____
_____
_____
_____
_____

Date Completed:_____

Overall Rating: ☆ ☆ ☆ ☆ ☆

Description:

_____
_____
_____
_____
_____

Why I wanted to do this:

_____
_____
_____

Thoughts/Memories:

_____
_____
_____
_____
_____
_____
_____
_____
_____
_____
_____
_____
_____

Date Completed:_____

Overall Rating: ☆ ☆ ☆ ☆ ☆

Description:

_____
_____
_____
_____
_____

Why I wanted to do this:

_____
_____
_____

Thoughts/Memories:

_____
_____
_____
_____
_____
_____
_____
_____
_____
_____
_____
_____

Date Completed:_____

Overall Rating: ☆ ☆ ☆ ☆ ☆

Description:

_____
_____
_____
_____
_____

Why I wanted to do this:

_____
_____
_____

Thoughts/Memories:

_____
_____
_____
_____
_____
_____
_____
_____
_____
_____
_____
_____
_____

Date Completed:_____

Overall Rating: ☆ ☆ ☆ ☆ ☆

Description:

_____
_____
_____
_____
_____

Why I wanted to do this:

_____
_____
_____

Thoughts/Memories:

_____
_____
_____
_____
_____
_____
_____
_____
_____
_____
_____
_____

Date Completed:_____

Overall Rating: ☆ ☆ ☆ ☆ ☆

Description:

_____
_____
_____
_____
_____

Why I wanted to do this:

_____
_____
_____

Thoughts/Memories:

_____
_____
_____
_____
_____
_____
_____
_____
_____
_____
_____
_____

Date Completed:_____

Overall Rating: ☆ ☆ ☆ ☆ ☆

Description:

_____

_____

_____

_____

_____

Why I wanted to do this:

_____

_____

_____

Thoughts/Memories:

_____

_____

_____

_____

_____

_____

_____

_____

_____

_____

_____

_____

Date Completed:_____

Overall Rating: ☆ ☆ ☆ ☆ ☆

Description:

_____
_____
_____
_____
_____

Why I wanted to do this:

_____
_____
_____

Thoughts/Memories:

_____
_____
_____
_____
_____
_____
_____
_____
_____
_____
_____
_____

Date Completed:_____

Overall Rating: ☆ ☆ ☆ ☆ ☆

Description:
_____
_____
_____
_____
_____

Why I wanted to do this:
_____
_____
_____

Thoughts/Memories:
_____
_____
_____
_____
_____
_____
_____
_____
_____
_____
_____
_____

Date Completed:_____

Overall Rating: ☆ ☆ ☆ ☆ ☆

Description:

_____
_____
_____
_____
_____

Why I wanted to do this:

_____
_____
_____

Thoughts/Memories:

_____
_____
_____
_____
_____
_____
_____
_____
_____
_____
_____
_____
_____

Date Completed:_____

Overall Rating: ☆ ☆ ☆ ☆ ☆

Description:

_____
_____
_____
_____
_____

Why I wanted to do this:

_____
_____
_____

Thoughts/Memories:

_____
_____
_____
_____
_____
_____
_____
_____
_____
_____
_____
_____

Date Completed:_____

Overall Rating: ☆ ☆ ☆ ☆ ☆

Description:

_____
_____
_____
_____
_____

Why I wanted to do this:

_____
_____
_____

Thoughts/Memories:

_____
_____
_____
_____
_____
_____
_____
_____
_____
_____
_____
_____
_____

Date Completed:_____

Overall Rating: ☆ ☆ ☆ ☆ ☆

Description:

_____
_____
_____
_____
_____

Why I wanted to do this:

_____
_____
_____

Thoughts/Memories:

_____
_____
_____
_____
_____
_____
_____
_____
_____
_____
_____
_____

Date Completed:_____

Overall Rating: ☆ ☆ ☆ ☆ ☆

Description:

_____
_____
_____
_____
_____

Why I wanted to do this:

_____
_____
_____

Thoughts/Memories:

_____
_____
_____
_____
_____
_____
_____
_____
_____
_____
_____
_____

Date Completed:_____

Overall Rating: ☆ ☆ ☆ ☆ ☆

Description:

_____
_____
_____
_____
_____

Why I wanted to do this:

_____
_____
_____

Thoughts/Memories:

_____
_____
_____
_____
_____
_____
_____
_____
_____
_____
_____
_____

Date Completed:_____

Overall Rating: ☆ ☆ ☆ ☆ ☆

Description:

_____
_____
_____
_____
_____

Why I wanted to do this:

_____
_____
_____

Thoughts/Memories:

_____
_____
_____
_____
_____
_____
_____
_____
_____
_____
_____
_____

Date Completed:_____

Overall Rating: ☆ ☆ ☆ ☆ ☆

Description:

_____
_____
_____
_____
_____

Why I wanted to do this:

_____
_____
_____

Thoughts/Memories:

_____
_____
_____
_____
_____
_____
_____
_____
_____
_____
_____
_____

Date Completed:_____

Overall Rating: ☆ ☆ ☆ ☆ ☆

Description:

_____
_____
_____
_____
_____

Why I wanted to do this:

_____
_____
_____

Thoughts/Memories:

_____
_____
_____
_____
_____
_____
_____
_____
_____
_____
_____
_____
_____

Date Completed:_____

Overall Rating: ☆ ☆ ☆ ☆ ☆

Description:

_____
_____
_____
_____
_____

Why I wanted to do this:

_____
_____
_____

Thoughts/Memories:

_____
_____
_____
_____
_____
_____
_____
_____
_____
_____
_____
_____

Date Completed:_____

Overall Rating: ☆ ☆ ☆ ☆ ☆

Description:

_____
_____
_____
_____
_____

Why I wanted to do this:

_____
_____
_____

Thoughts/Memories:

_____
_____
_____
_____
_____
_____
_____
_____
_____
_____
_____
_____

Date Completed: _____

Overall Rating: ☆ ☆ ☆ ☆ ☆

Description:

_____
_____
_____
_____
_____

Why I wanted to do this:

_____
_____
_____

Thoughts/Memories:

_____
_____
_____
_____
_____
_____
_____
_____
_____
_____
_____
_____
_____

Date Completed:_____

Overall Rating: ☆ ☆ ☆ ☆ ☆

Description:

_____
_____
_____
_____
_____

Why I wanted to do this:

_____
_____
_____

Thoughts/Memories:

_____
_____
_____
_____
_____
_____
_____
_____
_____
_____
_____
_____

Date Completed:_____

Overall Rating: ☆ ☆ ☆ ☆ ☆

Description:

_____
_____
_____
_____
_____

Why I wanted to do this:

_____
_____
_____

Thoughts/Memories:

_____
_____
_____
_____
_____
_____
_____
_____
_____
_____
_____
_____

Date Completed:_____

Overall Rating: ☆ ☆ ☆ ☆ ☆

Description:

_____
_____
_____
_____
_____

Why I wanted to do this:

_____
_____
_____

Thoughts/Memories:

_____
_____
_____
_____
_____
_____
_____
_____
_____
_____
_____
_____

Date Completed:_____

Overall Rating: ☆ ☆ ☆ ☆ ☆

Description:

_____
_____
_____
_____
_____

Why I wanted to do this:

_____
_____
_____

Thoughts/Memories:

_____
_____
_____
_____
_____
_____
_____
_____
_____
_____
_____
_____
_____

Date Completed:_____

Overall Rating: ☆ ☆ ☆ ☆ ☆

Description:

_____
_____
_____
_____
_____

Why I wanted to do this:

_____
_____
_____

Thoughts/Memories:

_____
_____
_____
_____
_____
_____
_____
_____
_____
_____
_____
_____

Date Completed:_____

Overall Rating: ☆ ☆ ☆ ☆ ☆

Description:

_____
_____
_____
_____
_____

Why I wanted to do this:

_____
_____
_____

Thoughts/Memories:

_____
_____
_____
_____
_____
_____
_____
_____
_____
_____
_____
_____
_____

Date Completed:_____

Overall Rating: ☆ ☆ ☆ ☆ ☆

Description:

_____
_____
_____
_____
_____

Why I wanted to do this:

_____
_____
_____

Thoughts/Memories:

_____
_____
_____
_____
_____
_____
_____
_____
_____
_____
_____
_____

Date Completed:_____

Overall Rating: ☆ ☆ ☆ ☆ ☆

Description:

_____
_____
_____
_____
_____

Why I wanted to do this:

_____
_____
_____

Thoughts/Memories:

_____
_____
_____
_____
_____
_____
_____
_____
_____
_____
_____
_____

Date Completed:_____

Overall Rating: ☆ ☆ ☆ ☆ ☆

Description:

_____

_____

_____

_____

_____

Why I wanted to do this:

_____

_____

_____

Thoughts/Memories:

_____

_____

_____

_____

_____

_____

_____

_____

_____

_____

_____

_____

Date Completed:_____

Overall Rating: ☆ ☆ ☆ ☆ ☆

Description:

_____
_____
_____
_____
_____

Why I wanted to do this:

_____
_____
_____

Thoughts/Memories:

_____
_____
_____
_____
_____
_____
_____
_____
_____
_____
_____
_____

Date Completed:_____

Overall Rating: ☆ ☆ ☆ ☆ ☆

Description:

_____
_____
_____
_____

Why I wanted to do this:

_____
_____
_____

Thoughts/Memories:

_____
_____
_____
_____
_____
_____
_____
_____
_____
_____
_____
_____

Date Completed:_____

Overall Rating: ☆ ☆ ☆ ☆ ☆

Description:

_____
_____
_____
_____
_____

Why I wanted to do this:

_____
_____
_____

Thoughts/Memories:

_____
_____
_____
_____
_____
_____
_____
_____
_____
_____
_____
_____
_____

Date Completed:_____

Overall Rating: ☆ ☆ ☆ ☆ ☆

Description:

_____
_____
_____
_____
_____

Why I wanted to do this:

_____
_____
_____

Thoughts/Memories:

_____
_____
_____
_____
_____
_____
_____
_____
_____
_____
_____
_____

Date Completed:_____

Overall Rating: ☆ ☆ ☆ ☆ ☆

Description:

_____
_____
_____
_____
_____

Why I wanted to do this:

_____
_____
_____

Thoughts/Memories:

_____
_____
_____
_____
_____
_____
_____
_____
_____
_____
_____
_____

Date Completed:_____

Overall Rating: ☆ ☆ ☆ ☆ ☆

Description:

_____
_____
_____
_____
_____

Why I wanted to do this:

_____
_____
_____

Thoughts/Memories:

_____
_____
_____
_____
_____
_____
_____
_____
_____
_____
_____
_____
_____

Date Completed:_____

Overall Rating: ☆ ☆ ☆ ☆ ☆

Description:

_____
_____
_____
_____
_____

Why I wanted to do this:

_____
_____
_____

Thoughts/Memories:

_____
_____
_____
_____
_____
_____
_____
_____
_____
_____
_____

Date Completed:_____

Overall Rating: ☆ ☆ ☆ ☆ ☆

Description:

_____
_____
_____
_____
_____

Why I wanted to do this:

_____
_____
_____

Thoughts/Memories:

_____
_____
_____
_____
_____
_____
_____
_____
_____
_____
_____
_____
_____

Date Completed:_____

Overall Rating: ☆ ☆ ☆ ☆ ☆

Description:
_____
_____
_____
_____
_____

Why I wanted to do this:
_____
_____
_____

Thoughts/Memories:
_____
_____
_____
_____
_____
_____
_____
_____
_____
_____
_____
_____
_____

Date Completed:_____

Overall Rating: ☆ ☆ ☆ ☆ ☆

Description:

_____
_____
_____
_____
_____

Why I wanted to do this:

_____
_____
_____

Thoughts/Memories:

_____
_____
_____
_____
_____
_____
_____
_____
_____
_____
_____
_____
_____

Date Completed:_____

Overall Rating: ☆ ☆ ☆ ☆ ☆

Description:

_____
_____
_____
_____
_____

Why I wanted to do this:

_____
_____
_____

Thoughts/Memories:

_____
_____
_____
_____
_____
_____
_____
_____
_____
_____
_____
_____
_____
_____

Date Completed:_____

Overall Rating: ☆ ☆ ☆ ☆ ☆

Description:

_____
_____
_____
_____
_____

Why I wanted to do this:

_____
_____
_____

Thoughts/Memories:

_____
_____
_____
_____
_____
_____
_____
_____
_____
_____
_____
_____

Date Completed:_____

Overall Rating: ☆ ☆ ☆ ☆ ☆

Description:

_____
_____
_____
_____
_____

Why I wanted to do this:

_____
_____
_____

Thoughts/Memories:

_____
_____
_____
_____
_____
_____
_____
_____
_____
_____
_____
_____
_____

Date Completed:_____

Overall Rating: ☆ ☆ ☆ ☆ ☆

Description:

_____
_____
_____
_____
_____

Why I wanted to do this:

_____
_____
_____

Thoughts/Memories:

_____
_____
_____
_____
_____
_____
_____
_____
_____
_____
_____
_____

Date Completed:_____

Overall Rating: ☆ ☆ ☆ ☆ ☆

Description:

_____
_____
_____
_____
_____

Why I wanted to do this:

_____
_____
_____

Thoughts/Memories:

_____
_____
_____
_____
_____
_____
_____
_____
_____
_____
_____
_____
_____

Date Completed:_____

Overall Rating: ☆ ☆ ☆ ☆ ☆

Description:

_____
_____
_____
_____
_____

Why I wanted to do this:

_____
_____
_____

Thoughts/Memories:

_____
_____
_____
_____
_____
_____
_____
_____
_____
_____
_____
_____
_____

Date Completed:_____

Overall Rating: ☆ ☆ ☆ ☆ ☆

Description:

_____
_____
_____
_____
_____

Why I wanted to do this:

_____
_____
_____

Thoughts/Memories:

_____
_____
_____
_____
_____
_____
_____
_____
_____
_____
_____
_____

Date Completed:_____

Overall Rating: ☆ ☆ ☆ ☆ ☆

Description:

_____
_____
_____
_____
_____

Why I wanted to do this:

_____
_____
_____

Thoughts/Memories:

_____
_____
_____
_____
_____
_____
_____
_____
_____
_____
_____
_____

Date Completed:_____

Overall Rating: ☆ ☆ ☆ ☆ ☆

Description:

_____
_____
_____
_____
_____

Why I wanted to do this:

_____
_____
_____

Thoughts/Memories:

_____
_____
_____
_____
_____
_____
_____
_____
_____
_____
_____
_____
_____

Date Completed:_____

Overall Rating: ☆ ☆ ☆ ☆ ☆

Description:

_____
_____
_____
_____
_____

Why I wanted to do this:

_____
_____
_____

Thoughts/Memories:

_____
_____
_____
_____
_____
_____
_____
_____
_____
_____
_____
_____
_____

Date Completed: _____

Overall Rating: ☆ ☆ ☆ ☆ ☆

Description:

_____

_____

_____

_____

_____

Why I wanted to do this:

_____

_____

_____

Thoughts/Memories:

_____

_____

_____

_____

_____

_____

_____

_____

_____

_____

_____

_____

Date Completed:_____

Overall Rating: ☆ ☆ ☆ ☆ ☆

Description:

_____
_____
_____
_____
_____

Why I wanted to do this:

_____
_____
_____

Thoughts/Memories:

_____
_____
_____
_____
_____
_____
_____
_____
_____
_____
_____
_____

Date Completed:_____

Overall Rating: ☆ ☆ ☆ ☆ ☆

Description:

_____
_____
_____
_____
_____

Why I wanted to do this:

_____
_____
_____

Thoughts/Memories:

_____
_____
_____
_____
_____
_____
_____
_____
_____
_____
_____
_____
_____

Date Completed:_____

Overall Rating: ☆ ☆ ☆ ☆ ☆

Description:

_____
_____
_____
_____
_____

Why I wanted to do this:

_____
_____
_____

Thoughts/Memories:

_____
_____
_____
_____
_____
_____
_____
_____
_____
_____
_____
_____

Date Completed:_____

Overall Rating: ☆ ☆ ☆ ☆ ☆

Description:

_____

_____

_____

_____

_____

Why I wanted to do this:

_____

_____

_____

Thoughts/Memories:

_____

_____

_____

_____

_____

_____

_____

_____

_____

_____

_____

_____

_____

_____

Date Completed:_____

Overall Rating: ☆ ☆ ☆ ☆ ☆

Description:

_____

_____

_____

_____

_____

Why I wanted to do this:

_____

_____

_____

Thoughts/Memories:

_____

_____

_____

_____

_____

_____

_____

_____

_____

_____

_____

_____

Date Completed:_____

Overall Rating: ☆ ☆ ☆ ☆ ☆

Description:
_____
_____
_____
_____
_____

Why I wanted to do this:
_____
_____
_____

Thoughts/Memories:
_____
_____
_____
_____
_____
_____
_____
_____
_____
_____
_____
_____

Date Completed:_____

Overall Rating: ☆ ☆ ☆ ☆ ☆

Description:

_____
_____
_____
_____
_____

Why I wanted to do this:

_____
_____
_____

Thoughts/Memories:

_____
_____
_____
_____
_____
_____
_____
_____
_____
_____
_____
_____
_____

Date Completed:_____

Overall Rating: ☆ ☆ ☆ ☆ ☆

Description:

_____

_____

_____

_____

_____

Why I wanted to do this:

_____

_____

_____

Thoughts/Memories:

_____

_____

_____

_____

_____

_____

_____

_____

_____

_____

_____

_____

Date Completed:_____

Overall Rating: ☆ ☆ ☆ ☆ ☆

Description:

_____
_____
_____
_____
_____

Why I wanted to do this:

_____
_____
_____

Thoughts/Memories:

_____
_____
_____
_____
_____
_____
_____
_____
_____
_____
_____
_____

Date Completed:_____

Overall Rating: ☆ ☆ ☆ ☆ ☆

Description:

_____
_____
_____
_____
_____

Why I wanted to do this:

_____
_____
_____

Thoughts/Memories:

_____
_____
_____
_____
_____
_____
_____
_____
_____
_____
_____
_____

Date Completed:_____

Overall Rating: ☆ ☆ ☆ ☆ ☆

Description:

_____
_____
_____
_____
_____

Why I wanted to do this:

_____
_____
_____

Thoughts/Memories:

_____
_____
_____
_____
_____
_____
_____
_____
_____
_____
_____
_____

Date Completed:_____

Overall Rating: ☆ ☆ ☆ ☆ ☆

Description:

_____
_____
_____
_____
_____

Why I wanted to do this:

_____
_____
_____

Thoughts/Memories:

_____
_____
_____
_____
_____
_____
_____
_____
_____
_____
_____
_____
_____

Date Completed:_____

Overall Rating: ☆ ☆ ☆ ☆ ☆

Description:

_____
_____
_____
_____
_____

Why I wanted to do this:

_____
_____
_____

Thoughts/Memories:

_____
_____
_____
_____
_____
_____
_____
_____
_____
_____
_____
_____
_____

Date Completed:_____

Overall Rating: ☆ ☆ ☆ ☆ ☆

Description:

_____

_____

_____

_____

_____

Why I wanted to do this:

_____

_____

_____

Thoughts/Memories:

_____

_____

_____

_____

_____

_____

_____

_____

_____

_____

_____

_____

Date Completed:_____

Overall Rating: ☆ ☆ ☆ ☆ ☆

Description:

_____
_____
_____
_____
_____

Why I wanted to do this:

_____
_____
_____

Thoughts/Memories:

_____
_____
_____
_____
_____
_____
_____
_____
_____
_____
_____
_____
_____

Date Completed:_____

Overall Rating: ☆ ☆ ☆ ☆ ☆

Description:

_____
_____
_____
_____
_____

Why I wanted to do this:

_____
_____
_____

Thoughts/Memories:

_____
_____
_____
_____
_____
_____
_____
_____
_____
_____
_____
_____

Date Completed:_____

Overall Rating: ☆ ☆ ☆ ☆ ☆

Description:

_____
_____
_____
_____
_____

Why I wanted to do this:

_____
_____
_____

Thoughts/Memories:

_____
_____
_____
_____
_____
_____
_____
_____
_____
_____
_____
_____

Date Completed:_____

Overall Rating: ☆ ☆ ☆ ☆ ☆

Description:

_____
_____
_____
_____
_____

Why I wanted to do this:

_____
_____
_____

Thoughts/Memories:

_____
_____
_____
_____
_____
_____
_____
_____
_____
_____
_____
_____

Date Completed:_____

Overall Rating: ☆ ☆ ☆ ☆ ☆

Description:

_____
_____
_____
_____
_____

Why I wanted to do this:

_____
_____
_____

Thoughts/Memories:

_____
_____
_____
_____
_____
_____
_____
_____
_____
_____
_____
_____

Date Completed:_____

Overall Rating: ☆ ☆ ☆ ☆ ☆

Description:

_____
_____
_____
_____
_____

Why I wanted to do this:

_____
_____
_____

Thoughts/Memories:

_____
_____
_____
_____
_____
_____
_____
_____
_____
_____
_____
_____
_____

Date Completed:_____

Overall Rating: ☆ ☆ ☆ ☆ ☆

Description:

_____
_____
_____
_____
_____

Why I wanted to do this:

_____
_____
_____

Thoughts/Memories:

_____
_____
_____
_____
_____
_____
_____
_____
_____
_____
_____
_____
_____

Date Completed:_____

Overall Rating: ☆ ☆ ☆ ☆ ☆

Description:

_____

_____

_____

_____

_____

Why I wanted to do this:

_____

_____

_____

Thoughts/Memories:

_____

_____

_____

_____

_____

_____

_____

_____

_____

_____

_____

_____

Date Completed:_____

Overall Rating: ☆ ☆ ☆ ☆ ☆

Description:

_____
_____
_____
_____
_____

Why I wanted to do this:

_____
_____
_____

Thoughts/Memories:

_____
_____
_____
_____
_____
_____
_____
_____
_____
_____
_____
_____
_____

Date Completed:_____

Overall Rating: ☆ ☆ ☆ ☆ ☆

Description:

_____
_____
_____
_____
_____

Why I wanted to do this:

_____
_____
_____

Thoughts/Memories:

_____
_____
_____
_____
_____
_____
_____
_____
_____
_____
_____
_____
_____

Date Completed:_____

Overall Rating: ☆ ☆ ☆ ☆ ☆

Description:

_____
_____
_____
_____
_____

Why I wanted to do this:

_____
_____
_____

Thoughts/Memories:

_____
_____
_____
_____
_____
_____
_____
_____
_____
_____
_____
_____
_____

Date Completed:_____

Overall Rating: ☆ ☆ ☆ ☆ ☆

Description:

_____
_____
_____
_____
_____

Why I wanted to do this:

_____
_____
_____

Thoughts/Memories:

_____
_____
_____
_____
_____
_____
_____
_____
_____
_____
_____
_____
_____

Date Completed:_____

Overall Rating: ☆ ☆ ☆ ☆ ☆

Description:

_____
_____
_____
_____
_____

Why I wanted to do this:

_____
_____
_____

Thoughts/Memories:

_____
_____
_____
_____
_____
_____
_____
_____
_____
_____
_____
_____

Date Completed:_____

Overall Rating: ☆ ☆ ☆ ☆ ☆

Description:

_____
_____
_____
_____
_____

Why I wanted to do this:

_____
_____
_____

Thoughts/Memories:

_____
_____
_____
_____
_____
_____
_____
_____
_____
_____
_____
_____
_____
_____

Date Completed:_____

Overall Rating: ☆ ☆ ☆ ☆ ☆

Description:

_____
_____
_____
_____
_____

Why I wanted to do this:

_____
_____
_____

Thoughts/Memories:

_____
_____
_____
_____
_____
_____
_____
_____
_____
_____
_____
_____

Date Completed:_____

Overall Rating: ☆ ☆ ☆ ☆ ☆

Description:

_____
_____
_____
_____
_____

Why I wanted to do this:

_____
_____
_____

Thoughts/Memories:

_____
_____
_____
_____
_____
_____
_____
_____
_____
_____
_____
_____

Date Completed:_____

Overall Rating: ☆ ☆ ☆ ☆ ☆

Description:
_____
_____
_____
_____
_____

Why I wanted to do this:
_____
_____
_____

Thoughts/Memories:
_____
_____
_____
_____
_____
_____
_____
_____
_____
_____
_____
_____

Date Completed:_____

Overall Rating: ☆ ☆ ☆ ☆ ☆

Description:

_____
_____
_____
_____
_____

Why I wanted to do this:

_____
_____
_____

Thoughts/Memories:

_____
_____
_____
_____
_____
_____
_____
_____
_____
_____
_____
_____

Date Completed:_____

Overall Rating: ☆ ☆ ☆ ☆ ☆

Description:

_____
_____
_____
_____
_____

Why I wanted to do this:

_____
_____
_____

Thoughts/Memories:

_____
_____
_____
_____
_____
_____
_____
_____
_____
_____
_____
_____
_____

Date Completed:_____

Overall Rating: ☆ ☆ ☆ ☆ ☆

Description:

_____

_____

_____

_____

_____

Why I wanted to do this:

_____

_____

_____

Thoughts/Memories:

_____

_____

_____

_____

_____

_____

_____

_____

_____

_____

_____

_____

Date Completed:_____

Overall Rating:　☆　☆　☆　☆　☆

Description:

_____
_____
_____
_____
_____

Why I wanted to do this:

_____
_____
_____

Thoughts/Memories:

_____
_____
_____
_____
_____
_____
_____
_____
_____
_____
_____
_____

Date Completed:_____

Overall Rating: ☆ ☆ ☆ ☆ ☆

Description:

_____
_____
_____
_____
_____

Why I wanted to do this:

_____
_____
_____

Thoughts/Memories:

_____
_____
_____
_____
_____
_____
_____
_____
_____
_____
_____
_____

Date Completed:_____

Overall Rating: ☆ ☆ ☆ ☆ ☆

Description:

_____
_____
_____
_____
_____

Why I wanted to do this:

_____
_____
_____

Thoughts/Memories:

_____
_____
_____
_____
_____
_____
_____
_____
_____
_____
_____
_____
_____

Date Completed:_____

Overall Rating: ☆ ☆ ☆ ☆ ☆

Description:

_____
_____
_____
_____

Why I wanted to do this:

_____
_____
_____

Thoughts/Memories:

_____
_____
_____
_____
_____
_____
_____
_____
_____
_____
_____
_____